SECRET
MISSIONS

SECRET MISSIONS

Ellen Levine

SCHOLASTIC INC.
New York Toronto London Auckland Sydney

Acknowledgments

Special thanks to the Research Desk and the Co-operative Services Division of the New York Public Library for their help in my search for special materials about Lydia Darragh and William Still.

And particularly warm thanks to Leesha Rose for allowing me to retell her story.

ISBN 0-590-41183-7

Copyright © 1988 by Ellen Levine.
All rights reserved. Published by Scholastic Inc.

12 11 10 9 8 7 6 5 4 3 2   9/8 0 1 2 3/9

Printed in the U.S.A.   11

First Scholastic printing, August 1988

Dedication

In memory of Madam Francisca Halamajowa and her daughter, Hela, Christians who once lived in Sokal, Russia. For nearly two years, at great personal risk, they hid my Jewish relatives on their land and saved them from extermination by the Nazi forces that occupied the town.

CONTENTS

Author's Preface

This book is about four heroes. Often we think heroes are so unusual, we could never be like them. But they can be people like our neighbors, our friends, our parents, even ourselves.

The heroes in this book risked prison, even death, for what they believed in.

Lydia Darragh, born in Ireland, moved to America. She wasn't paid to spy for the American revolutionary army. It wasn't her job. In fact, we aren't sure George Washington even knew her name. But we can be sure he was grateful for the information she supplied.

Alexander Ross, a Canadian, a white man, thought slavery was so terrible that he risked his life in a foreign country, the United States, to help others.

William Still, son of slaves, was born free himself. Nonetheless, he devoted his life to helping free others.

Leesha Bos, a Jew, survived the Nazi occupation in Holland. She joined the Resistance movement to free her country and her people.

These four lives span a period of over two hundred years, from the 1700's to the present. But all have certain things in common: quick thinking, generous hearts, and the courage to undertake secret missions.

LYDIA DARRAGH
Revolutionary Spy

Was she an American spy? A British officer questions Lydia Darragh.

Lydia Darragh

"Not My House"

The British marched into Philadelphia one September day in 1777. They took over the city, including Independence Hall and many private homes. Now they wanted Lydia Darragh's house. This was a mistake they would live to regret.

Lydia was upset as she cleared the plates from the kitchen table. The British officer who had just left was probably twenty-two years old, like her son Charles who was also an officer, but in the American army. Both seemed too young to be soldiers in a war, too young to face the dangers of battle and the danger of death.

Lydia stopped herself. If she kept on, she'd have to think about her Quaker religion, which said you shouldn't fight in a war, you shouldn't join in any violence. But Charles had felt so strongly that the colonists should be independent from English rule that he had become a soldier. She had been troubled when he first had told her about his plans. But their religion also taught that you must be true to your beliefs. Charles was brave to stick to what he believed in.

She put aside these troubling questions. Right now, she had a more immediate problem. The officer had come to say that Sir William Howe, the Commander in Chief of all the British forces, wanted *her* home for his staff officers.

She took off her apron and went to the front hall to get her coat — her long, gray, comfortable coat that kept her warm down to her ankles. Simple Quaker clothes — no ruffles, no frills — had always given her a quiet feeling of peace and calm. And now in her Quaker wraps, this small, neat woman was off to do battle with a general.

It was a chilly day. The sun was hidden behind heavy clouds, and Lydia was glad she didn't have far to walk. Howe's headquarters were almost across the street from her own home. She hated to see these redcoats in what was once the Cadwalader house. Mr. Cadwalader had enlisted in General George Washington's army, she had heard. And the very enemy he was fighting had taken over his home.

When she entered the Cadwalader house, Lydia approached an officer and stated her name and business.

"I am Lydia Darragh of 177 South Second Street, and I have been told General Howe wants to take over my home. If that is so, sir, I must protest. Not my house! My husband and I and our children have lived there many years, and I do not think it fair or proper to turn us out."

The officer listened and then introduced himself.

"Captain William Barrington, Ma'am. I'm

sure the general wouldn't have requested anything we don't absolutely need, but I'll tell him you're here."

When he returned, he said the general could not see her now, but perhaps tomorrow. He added that he doubted the general would change his order.

As she turned to leave, Lydia said, "I beg your pardon, Captain, but are you from Dublin?"

"Indeed, yes," he replied with a smile. Lydia Darragh had been Lydia Barrington before she had married. She, too, had grown up in Ireland. And as they talked, it seemed that they were probably distant cousins.

The next morning a British officer knocked on the Darragh door with a sharp rap. He delivered his message quickly.

"General Howe will grant your request to remain in your house. However, he requires a room to be available at all times for his use."

With great relief Lydia said, "May I inquire for what purpose, so that I can properly prepare the room?" The officer explained

6

that the British needed a council room for meetings and that the room was to be made ready immediately.

In the weeks that passed, Lydia often wondered if her "cousin" had managed to persuade the general to allow them to remain in their home. If Captain Barrington had done so, he probably would have argued to the general that from her clothing it was clear that the Darraghs were Quakers. The British would have nothing to fear. Everyone knew Quakers didn't fight in wars.

What the British didn't know, of course, was that one Darragh son *was* fighting in the war. And, more important, that his mother was prepared to help him.

Button Up

Officers from British headquarters came in and out of the Darragh house at all hours. Their meetings were usually brief, and Lydia was asked only to leave candles and to start a fire in the hearth. Often she would see British officers in the streets as she went about her daily chores. Lydia was a soft-spoken, gentle person with whom people felt comfortable.

She never seemed to ask questions, yet officers told her all kinds of information. She was such an ordinary person, they thought, what harm could there be in mentioning, for instance, that a certain division of the army was moving nearer to Philadelphia, and how nice it would be to see one's friends? Or that the ship that had arrived yesterday had brought in a load of biscuits — not so tasty, and, by the way, also a certain number of new weapons. She'd just nod and smile and wish them a good day.

When the British took the room in the Darragh house, Lydia and her husband William sent their youngest children to the home of Mr. Darragh's cousins in the country. John, who was fourteen years old, and Ann, who was twenty-one, remained with their parents in Philadelphia.

William Darragh was a tutor. He had been a private teacher for Lydia's family in Ireland. That's how they had met. He continued to teach in America after they had married and moved to Philadelphia.

Besides basic school subjects, William taught some students shorthand, a fast way of making a few marks that stood for words and sentences. To someone who didn't know shorthand, the marks looked like meaningless scratches on a piece of paper. William always used shorthand as a fast and convenient way to make notes on what he had read or on what someone had said.

One evening as Lydia sat sewing by the kitchen fire, she thought about the information she had heard earlier that day. Movement of troops was surely something the American army would want to know about. But how to get the information to them?

"Mother, I lost a button," John said as he showed her his coat. "It must have come off when I crawled through the brush before I reached Nicetown Lane."

John had sneaked through the British lines to visit his older brother Charles, who was camped with the American army north of the British forces. Lydia was greatly relieved that nothing worse had happened to John than the loss of a button.

As she rummaged through her sewing basket for a button mold to use in making a new button, Lydia suddenly looked up and said, "John, please ask your father to come quickly." William came in still holding the book he had been reading.

"William, will you write this sentence in shorthand?" she asked. "On Tuesday last, a division of three hundred soldiers joined General Howe's troops at the western section."

William Darragh left to get his pen and paper. He returned with a very small square of paper on which he had made his shorthand marks. Lydia folded it up into an even smaller piece and fitted it on top of the button mold. Then she cut a piece of material from inside John's coat where it wouldn't be missed and stitched it over the button. When she sewed the button to the coat, it looked like all the others. You'd never know it had a piece of paper folded up inside of it.

William and John watched in fascination. No one said anything when Lydia finished. They just sat looking at each other.

"Dare we send John with this?" Lydia finally asked her husband. "If he's caught —

I can't bear to think what the British would do." William nodded. No one could guarantee the safety of prisoners of war. Some who had been caught were never again seen alive.

In a soft voice John said, "Mother, Father, I want to do this. This information may be important not only for the American army, but also for Charles."

"He might live or die by what we learn," Lydia added. Again there was silence. Then John looked at his father and laughed.

"You always told Charles that learning shorthand would help him someday. Wait till he sees how!"

When William put out the candles a short while later, each one went up to bed lost in thought.

The next morning when John arose, he found a small package of bread and cheese by his plate at the breakfast table — food for his long day's trip to the American lines, Lydia said. John was both nervous and excited, but as William and Lydia kissed him good-bye, they felt only fear.

That was seven o'clock in the morning. Charles's camp was about twelve miles away. Some of the way would be on open road, once John got past the British lines. The rest was through bushes, fields, and woods. Lydia watched the afternoon and evening hours slip by. She knew she shouldn't worry until after seven or eight P.M.

At seven fifteen in the evening the front door opened and a tired but smiling John came into the kitchen. He gave each of his parents a long hug.

"I'm hungry!" He laughed and added, "By the way, Mother, I seem to have lost a button on my coat. Would you make me another?"

Lydia told John that on later trips he must bring the button mold home. In these days of war shortages, she didn't want to run out of buttons. And after all, who knew how many she'd need?

"Victory Is Certain"

It was icy cold on Tuesday morning, December 2, when a British officer knocked at the Darragh door. A gust of chilling wind came in with him. As he stepped into the hallway, the officer looked at Lydia and said in a very serious tone, "Mrs. Darragh, we must meet in the council room this evening. This is a very important meeting, and we wish that your family be in bed by eight P.M. This meeting must be held without interruption."

Never before had the British issued such an order to Lydia, and she felt herself getting hot with anger. But she held her tongue and thought, You are not very wise, young man. You have made me extremely curious about your "important" meeting.

Instead, all she said was, "Will you be needing anything for your meeting?"

"Only candles and a fire in the hearth," he replied and turned to leave.

He paused at the door, turned, and repeated, "You must all be in bed by eight. When we are finished, someone will awaken you so that you can put out the fire and lock the front door after us." Lydia merely nodded.

Lydia had a great deal to do that day and didn't prepare for the British meeting until after dinner. That's when she told the rest of the family that the British wanted everyone in bed by eight. There was some grumbling about having to take orders from the redcoats. Lydia set the candles in the holders and asked John to start the fire going in the council room.

A few minutes before eight o'clock that evening, Lydia answered the knock at the front door and let in a group of British officers. The other Darraghs had already gone to their rooms. In fact, William was half asleep when Lydia came into their room and whispered, "Good-night."

She was too wide awake to be able to fall asleep. She lay in bed thinking about the British meeting down the hall. That officer in the morning had been insistent that everyone go to bed early. What could they be talking about that was so important, she wondered?

Lydia lay awake for at least an hour. She felt a presence of evil, she later told her daughter, a sense that something terrible was about to happen. Without planning to, she found herself standing on the cold floorboards. She took her bed robe from the chair and quietly opened the door of her room. The floor under her bare feet creaked slightly. She held her breath, heard nothing, and moved very slowly down the hall.

There was a light from under the door of the council room, and Lydia heard the murmur of voices. But she couldn't tell what anyone was saying. She opened the door of a closet next to the council room. The inside wall of the closet was also the wall of the meeting room. It was made of very thin board covered with paper. With her ear pressed to the wall, she could hear the voices clearly.

"And so, gentlemen, the plan is that the forces will march out late Thursday night. Washington's troops at White Marsh are disorganized. They will be totally unprepared for our attack. With our superior forces, victory is certain!"

Lydia gasped aloud and then quickly covered her mouth. Had they heard her? Would they find her? The voices continued. She was still safe. Numbers, they were talking about numbers. Troops, cannon, boats on wheels. Chairs scraped the floor. The meeting was ending. Lydia quickly left the closet and tiptoed to her room. She was barely under the covers when she heard a knock at her door.

"Mrs. Darragh?" the officer called softly. She lay in bed, afraid to answer too quickly.

He called out again and then a third time.

"Mrs. Darragh?"

This time she rose, went to the door, and whispered, "Yes?"

"We're leaving now, so you can lock the door. Good-night."

Lydia waited a few minutes until she heard the front door close. Then she locked it and went to put out the fire. Back in bed, her head reeling from what she had heard, she finally fell into a troubled sleep.

A Sack of Flour

The next morning Lydia was particularly quiet at the breakfast table. When William asked if she felt well, she simply said it had taken her a long time to fall asleep.

As she went about her chores, she wasn't certain what she should do. The British attack plan was the most important piece of information she had ever gotten. She had always talked with William about important matters. But this — this was so dangerous that if William knew, he, too, would be in danger. It was better not to tell him, she thought. And it was definitely too dangerous to send John with this news.

All day she thought about how to get the information to General Washington's head-quarters. She could try to find Charles, but John had said Charles's camp was moving.

The tavern called the Rising Sun was an American headquarters Charles had told them about. Perhaps she could get there. It was eight or nine miles away. But first she had to get through the British lines. She couldn't crawl through brush or wander in the woods like John. She needed an official way.

From a kitchen table drawer she took a folded piece of paper. It was a pass she had gotten from British headquarters just the week before. The pass allowed her to go through the British lines to the Frankford flour mill about five and a half miles from her home. It was in a no-man's land, with the British troops on one side and the Americans on the other.

She smiled to herself, thinking, that's a good reason. Here it is, December third, the holidays are coming, and I have a lot of baking to do.

When William came home that evening, she told him she was going the next day to the Frankford mill. William didn't like the idea of Lydia going between the army lines. He urged her to take along the young girl who sometimes helped in the house.

"Oh, no," said Lydia. "No need for that. I'll be fine," she insisted.

The next day, Lydia left 177 South Second Street early in the morning. She carried her empty flour sack and showed her pass when she came to the British patrol at the outskirts of the city. It was a bitter cold day, and she trudged through patches of snow and mud. When she reached the Frankford mill, she left her bag there, telling the miller she had other business and would be back later.

That old mill had stood there nearly eighty years. Although she was only forty-eight years old, Lydia herself was beginning to feel like eighty. Weak and dizzy as the chill wind cut through her, she continued to walk along Nicetown Lane in the direction of the Rising Sun tavern.

Hoofbeats stopped sharply in front of her. As the officer peered down, he smiled in recognition.

"Why Mrs. Darragh, what are you doing so far from home?" Lydia looked up into the face of young Thomas Craig, lieutenant colonel in the American Army. She had known his family for years.

"Hello, Thomas. I haven't seen Charles for a long time, and since I was at the Frankford mill, I thought I'd try to find his camp."

Craig dismounted and walked beside her, taking her arm.

"You seem very tired, Mrs. Darragh," he said.

She looked closely at him and said, "Please, Thomas, may I speak plainly with you?"

"Of course," he replied, never expecting for one moment what he was about to hear.

Lydia leaned on his arm for support and said, "I have information for General Washington. General Howe is planning an attack on White Marsh with five thousand men, thirteen pieces of cannon, baggage wagons, and eleven boats on wagon wheels. They are starting out late tonight." She explained how she had learned of this and then said, "You must make a solemn promise never to reveal my name."

Craig immediately understood the dangers she faced and gave his word. He insisted on taking her to the nearby farmhouse of a friend to rest.

Lydia was relieved as she watched him from the kitchen window of the farmhouse. She had passed on the information. The warm milk and bread were comforting, but a troubling thought nagged at her. What if something happened to the lieutenant? What if he didn't get to General Washington in time? Perhaps she should get the message to the Rising Sun as well.

Sometime later, a woman walked into the Rising Sun tavern. It was filled with American soldiers. The woman asked to speak to the commanding officer and was directed to General Boudinout. He spent hours every day at the tavern gathering information from the surrounding country-side about the movements of the British. The woman asked for a pass to go to the Frankford mill.

As she spoke, she handed him a small sewing case, looked at him carefully, and then quickly turned away. The case had many small pockets, all of which were empty — until he came to the last one, that is. Rolled up inside of it was a small tube of paper. When he opened it, he read, "Howe to White Marsh Dec. 4, 5,000 men, 13 cannon, baggage wagons, 11 boats on wagon wheels." When he looked up, the woman was gone. He never had a chance to ask her name.

"A Parcel of Fools"

The flour sack got heavier with each mile. Lydia Darragh reached home about nine P.M. on the very night the British were to march out of Philadelphia. After a quick supper, when everyone had gone to bed, Lydia sat by the kitchen window. In the far distance she heard the British army drum roll. They were on the march. She wondered if the Americans had had time enough to prepare for the attack.

She had to wait four days for the answer. Each day as she walked through the streets going about her business, she listened for comments about the British troops. She didn't dare ask any questions. A few soldiers remained in the city at the headquarters, and she chatted with them and listened, but learned nothing. At eleven A.M. Monday, December 8, British troops began straggling back into the city. She watched them all day, not knowing what had happened and still not daring to ask.

The next evening before dinner, a British officer came to the door. He walked in and said, "Mrs. Darragh, please come with me. I wish to talk with you."

His tone was sharp as he headed for the council room. Lydia's heart pounded fiercely. What did he want to talk to her about? Had they found out what she had done? Had she been betrayed? Her hands were cold and her face hot. The officer closed the council room door, walked to the table in the middle of the room, and turned toward her. Fortunately it was dark in the room, and he couldn't really see her face.

"Was your family all in bed the night of

our meeting last Thursday?" he asked.

"Yes," she replied. She didn't have to lie — everybody *had* been in bed.

"I need not ask about you," he said. "I know you were asleep for I knocked on your door three times before you heard me."

Lydia bit her lip as she listened.

"But one thing is certain," he continued. "The enemy knew we were coming and were prepared for us. I can't imagine who told General Washington about our plans, unless the walls of this house could speak." He paused and then went on.

"When we arrived near White Marsh, we found all their cannon and troops ready. We've been forced to march back like a parcel of fools!" he said angrily. Then he left.

Lydia could barely contain her joy. The American forces had not been defeated! In fact, they had forced the British to retreat. All she said at dinner was that it seemed the British had suffered a defeat. The Darraghs took no pleasure in warfare, but they smiled quietly, trusting that Charles was still safe and that the American fight for independence was still alive.

Nine months after they had marched into Philadelphia, the British marched out. One June day in 1778, Lydia stood in front of her house and watched them leave. Her youngest children would soon be back in their room, for the British would no longer be using it.

And now, for the first time, she felt it was safe to tell William what she had done on that cold December fourth. Although her voice was calm as she spoke, both of them knew the grave danger she had faced. But that was over now. Lydia was safe, and Philadelphia was once again in the hands of the Americans.

ALEXANDER ROSS
Man in Disguise

Alexander Ross helped many slaves escape. He became a
famous naturalist in his later years.

"It's a Command"

The black man on the stage spoke in a clear, strong voice. He was a runaway slave from America. He described his life on a plantation in the South. Hunger, work, little sleep, frequent punishments — day after day after day. Then, in the middle of his talk, he suddenly turned his back to the audience and pulled his shirt up. Everybody gasped.

A young man named Alexander Ross was in that audience in a small town in Canada. His throat tightened in shock and anger — the man's back was covered with scars from whippings by his owner. Years later Alex-

31

ander could squeeze his eyes shut and still picture that scene.

Not too long after that lecture, a book about slavery in America was published. The year was 1852, and everybody, it seemed, was reading it, even in Canada.

Even Alexander. He closed the book quietly and looked at the cover title: *Uncle Tom's Cabin* by Harriet Beecher Stowe. In his mind he could picture the slave cabins, the old people, the children, and the families split up after slave sales. Above all, he thought about the slaves who had escaped and the people who had helped them. How brave they all were.

Suddenly his heart began to beat quickly. It sounded so loud, he could barely hear the words in his head.

I must help the slaves become free. It's a command, he thought. This book is a command!

Alexander's mother believed firmly that slavery was wrong, and she had many friends who were abolitionists. They wanted to get rid of slavery, and they raised money to send to antislavery groups in America.

Mrs. Ross had a good friend named Gerrit Smith. Mr. Smith lived in New York State and made frequent trips to Canada, where he sometimes visited Alexander's home. At night, drinking a cup of tea in the Ross kitchen, Gerrit Smith talked about the antislavery movement in America. And Alexander listened carefully.

When Mr. Smith next came to visit, Alexander wanted to know more about *Uncle Tom's Cabin*.

"Mrs. Stowe changed the names and places, but the kinds of things she described have really happened," Gerrit said. "She wrote a magazine article about it because so many people asked her if slavery was really as terrible as the book said."

Alexander had a hard time falling asleep that night. He planned to talk with Mr. Smith the next day about going to New York and working on the Underground Railroad. That's what they called it in America, and what a

wonderful and mysterious sound it had —
a railroad underground! Not a real train, of
course, but a secret network of people helping fugitive slaves escape from the South to
freedom in the North.

Learning the Ropes

The air was crisp, and Alexander felt excited as he got out of the carriage in front of Gerrit Smith's home. The smell of apples cooking in the Smith kitchen was a warm welcome.

Alexander had come to learn how the Underground Railroad worked — to find out who helped the fugitive slaves, where the "safe houses" were, the routes, and what he himself could do to help.

After dinner that first night, Gerrit took him to the house of a friend who also worked on the Underground Railroad. The two men explained to Alexander the secret travel system for helping fugitive blacks escape. People who hid runaway slaves in their homes were called "station masters" and "station mistresses." And their houses were the "stations." If you took runaways in your wagon from one station to another, you were a "conductor."

"By the way, Alexander, what do you think of this collection of books?" Gerrit pointed to a bookcase in the corner of the living room next to the fireplace. Alexander wondered why Gerrit had changed the subject, but he went to the bookcase and pulled a book from a shelf.

Gerrit walked over quietly and leaned against the fireplace. Startled, Alexander watched as the bookcase slid to the side, revealing a hidden door.

"You wanted to know how the Underground Railroad works. Well, this is one way," Gerrit smiled as he pointed to the nearly hidden button on the side of the fireplace. The other man opened the secret door. It led to a narrow passageway and down a staircase into a hiding place in the cellar for runaway slaves.

"If you go down to the basement through the regular cellar door, you won't see the hidden room," he said. "The only way into the secret room is through the passageway behind the bookcase."

In the days that passed, Gerrit told Alexander about the farmhouses, the barns, the small sheds in the woods, that all were hiding places for runaway slaves. It seemed there was a network of these safe houses throughout the North as well as the South, so that slave hunters who were tracking down fugitives wouldn't catch them and take them back to their owners.

Alexander stayed with Gerrit Smith through the winter and spent hours memorizing the maps of all the roads to freedom. In the early spring, they traveled to Philadelphia. Alexander planned to head south from that city to begin helping slaves who wanted to escape.

Meeting at the home of some friends, he learned about the many real dangers of working on the Underground Railroad.

"Prison is the least of it, my boy," said one person. "If you're caught, hanging's more likely."

"Some say you're lucky if you're shot and die immediately," said another.

"We've heard stories of beatings and whippings," said a third.

An old gentleman urged Alexander to stay in the North and help the antislavery cause in other ways. There were so many important things to do — letters to write, money to raise, public speeches to give. But Alexander remembered the scarred back of that exslave that he had seen in Canada.

"Look what *they* have faced," he said, speaking of the black people he had met at home. "If these women and men are willing to risk their lives and the lives of their children to be free, I, too, can take risks to help."

The First Escapes

Alexander left Philadelphia on an April morning in 1857 to begin his dangerous work. He planned to start in Virginia, where he would stay with a Quaker family.

He had learned that many station masters and conductors on the Underground Railroad were Quakers, also known as Friends. The Quaker religion taught that no person had a right to own another person and that if the law said slavery was fine, then the law was wrong.

On the way to Richmond, Alexander read a Virginia newspaper. There were stories about the price of cotton and about towns in the West where settlers were fighting about bringing in slaves. There were also several articles about runaway slaves. Thousands of blacks had already escaped from southern plantations and farms. Nobody knew exactly how many. And slave owners were very angry. They called whites who helped the slaves "Negro thieves." Years later Alexander would say that he was as proud of that title as any a king could grant him.

Every day the papers had notices about escaped slaves. Owners offered money to anyone who would return a fugitive:

"$75 reward. Runaway — my man George; has holes in his ears; is marked on the back with a whip; has a scar on the forehead."

Alexander grew especially angry when he saw the newspaper advertisements offering slaves for sale: children, ages eight, nine, ten or older; infants, some only a month old; teenagers, parents, aunts and uncles, grandparents — it seemed these slave owners sold people the way they sold their mules and cows and hogs!

He walked from the train station to the Friend's house, where he was welcomed. All he had with him was a small suitcase and a revolver he carried in his pocket in case he had to protect himself.

Alexander spent the first week making his plans. He decided he would rent a horse and ride into the Virginia countryside, where he'd pass by plantations. He wasn't exactly sure how he would get to talk with slaves, but he was anxious to begin.

Sunday morning he went out riding. On a dusty, deserted lane, he thought he heard singing in the distance. He tied his horse to a fence post and walked through the woods to a clearing where a group of about thirty slaves was holding a church service.

The singing stopped as he approached, and the group stared at him. Finally, the preacher, an elderly, gray-haired black man, spoke to him.

"Good morning, sir."

Alexander smiled and greeted the group in return. He asked if he could stay for the rest of the service.

There was a silence and then the preacher said slowly, "You're welcome to pray with us."

At the end of the service, Alexander walked with the preacher a little away from the group. The old man had a clear, strong gaze and a gentle smile. Alexander decided that he must take a chance with this man.

"I've come from Canada," he said, "and I want to help any of your people who wish to escape there. May I talk with your friends?"

The preacher looked long and hard at him. Was this white man to be trusted? Or was this a trap set by the plantation owners to stop the escapes? Dare he believe this man who spoke with a strange accent?

"What is it you want to do?" he said, finally. And Alexander told him. He would tell the group about life in the North and give directions to any who wanted to escape.

The old man listened carefully, and then they went back to the group. Alexander explained to everyone what he had told the preacher. He spoke of the dangers of escaping.

At the end he said, "I know you want to think about it. I know it is a very difficult decision." He looked carefully from face to face. "You may become free, but you may die trying to get there. I'll come back here next Sunday evening to give the details to any of you who want to try." Then he shook hands with everyone and left. As he was heading home, he wondered if anybody would show up the following week.

The next Sunday, nine people waited for him in the growing darkness. They listened closely to the instructions he gave: Travel only at night. Rest during the day in safe places — either in houses of friends or hidden in the woods. Don't build any fires if you can possibly help it. Walk in the streams and creeks to keep the bloodhounds from being able to smell your tracks.

Then he gave them the names of people who would help along the route. They repeated the names slowly and carefully, memorizing everything. Then Alexander opened his pack and gave out compasses, small packets of food that would last a few days, and a few pocket knives that he had brought. They all whispered "Good luck!" to each other and then slipped quietly away into the night.

When he got back to where he was staying, Alexander wrote letters to friends in Pennsylvania, Indiana, and Ohio. He used the code he had worked out with them. "I've sent nine packages of hardware," which meant nine men might be arriving. "Dry goods" was the code for women. Then he signed the letters with a phony name.

The next day he left for Nashville, Tennessee, where he found another black church group and helped seven young men to escape. He gave them compasses, twenty dollars to the leader, as much food as they could carry, one pistol, and three knives. As he wrote to his friends, more packages of hardware were on their way.

Memphis was the next stop. Alexander was very tired when he checked into a hotel early in the afternoon. Barely taking the time to remove his shoes, he fell asleep on the couch in his room. About an hour later he was awakened by the shouts of a newsboy outside the hotel window, "SLAVES ESCAPE FROM NASHVILLE!"

He rushed to the window and yelled down for the boy to bring up a paper. The article described each of the slaves he had helped to escape. Their owners were offering a three-hundred-dollar reward for each one of them.

And then Alexander caught his breath. The slave owners were offering a reward of twelve hundred dollars for the capture of the person who had helped the fugitives. *Him!* They wanted him. He had to admit that they described him fairly well — light-colored hair, mustache and beard, tweed suit. He looked in the mirror and for the first time he was really frightened.

That night a man in a dark jacket and pants, no mustache, no beard, boarded a ship traveling north on the Mississippi River. As Alexander stood watching the reflection of the stars on the water, he thought, I, *too*, am a package of hardware headed for safety!

"I'd Rather Be Dead"

Alexander remained in the North for several months with antislavery friends until the excitement about the Richmond and Nashville escapes died down. In December, he planned his second trip, this time to the deep South.

Early one morning he boarded a steamship in New York City bound for New Orleans, Louisiana. Again, all he had with him was a small suitcase. But this time he had a special plan. Ever since childhood, Alexander had loved to spend time in the woods. Before he was ten, he knew the names of thirty birds and could identify many different flowers. What more perfect disguise than to be a naturalist, traveling in the South to study birds and flowers!

He stayed in New Orleans for a short time preparing his disguise. He had a sketch pad, notebooks, and a shotgun. He also carried materials for preserving bird skins. All these things were organized in a bag he carried over his shoulder. Then he left for Vicksburg, Mississippi.

There he rented a room in a private home, explaining to everyone he met that he was studying the flowers and birds of Mississippi. He rode into the countryside and introduced himself to plantation owners, asking if he could walk through their woods and fields to study nature.

He was very convincing. He showed them his drawings and named the different birds and flowers he had identified. Often he was invited into the slave owners' homes for lunch or dinner. After such a meal, they would send one of their slaves to accompany Alexander as he toured their land.

This was *exactly* what Alexander wanted. He'd talk with the slave and get to know him a little. If Alexander felt the man could be trusted, he would explain his true purpose.

Fortunately, he never made a mistake in his judgments about whom to tell. Then Alexander would ask the man to arrange a meeting with others who wanted to travel on the Underground Railroad. After helping with two or three such escapes, Alexander would quietly pack his bag and leave town.

One day, having traveled this way for several months, he reached the city of Columbus, Mississippi. Again, he introduced himself as a naturalist to the plantation owners in the surrounding countryside.

Late one afternoon he found himself drinking tea in the home of a very cruel man. The man boasted to Alexander that he branded his slaves with his own initials so that they'd be easy to identify if they ever tried to run away. It was hard for Alexander to hide his anger.

"We're fortunate in the North not to have

slaves, so we don't have to worry about escapes," was all he said.

During this conversation, one of the slaves was serving a plate of cakes. The black man listened carefully as Alexander talked about the North. When the owner offered Alexander the services of one of his slaves, this man volunteered.

"Colonel, sir," he said to his owner, "if you want me to . . ."

The owner didn't even look at him, but turned to Alexander and said, "My man Joe here will go with you."

"Now take care you mind what Mr. Ross wants," he snapped at Joe.

Early on a Friday morning, Alexander arrived at the plantation and started walking with Joe through the fields. Joe told him about his life and his great desire to escape to the North. Alexander explained the dangers — hunger, terrifying packs of dogs giving chase, capture, and possibly even death. Joe looked at him and said in almost a whisper, "Mr. Ross, I'd rather be dead than stay a slave."

"Arrest That Man!"

On Saturday Alexander again visited the plantation and went hiking with Joe. This time he gave Joe the names of station masters in Ohio and Indiana, and also handed him a compass and knife. When Alexander left the planatation and returned to his hotel, he thought to himself that Joe seemed to be a smart and careful man. He hoped he would succeed in escaping.

Two days later Alexander sat in the hotel dining room finishing his evening meal. He heard loud talking in the next room. Suddenly the hotel owner rushed into the room and said, "A gentleman wants to talk with you." From the sound of the voices, Alexander didn't think the visitor was a gentleman. Scarcely had he risen from the table, when the door was shoved open and Joe's owner, the colonel, stormed in.

"That's him, that's the one!" he shouted, pointing at Alexander. A crowd pushed into the room. The colonel yelled, "Arrest that man!"

The sheriff stepped forward, grabbed Alexander's arm, and said, "You're my prisoner."

The words were chilling. Alexander knew the laws in Mississippi. You could be imprisoned for up to twenty years or put to death for helping slaves escape. He tried to keep his voice calm.

"Why are you arresting me?" he asked.

The colonel shook his fist in Alexander's face. "You cursed abolitionist!" he snarled. "My man Joe hasn't been seen since Saturday when he was out with you!"

The men in the room were angry. They had had enough of runaway slaves. Now

they believed they had finally caught someone who was helping the fugitives. They
glared at Ross and began to press in toward
him.

Someone in the back yelled, "Let's get us
some rope!"

"Hang him!" another shouted. Alexander
was put in handcuffs, the colonel cursing all
the while.

As they hustled him out of the room,
Alexander spoke. "You say I broke your laws.
But will you act like cowards and let this
man get you to murder me? Or are you brave
men, willing to give me a fair trial?" He
didn't really believe he would get a fair trial,
but if there was a trial at all, at least he'd
live for a little while longer.

First one, then several people shouted,
"Try him! Give him his trial!"

Alexander was kept overnight in a filthy
jail. The next morning the sheriff brought
him into a courtroom. The colonel spoke
first and told his story. He demanded that
Alexander be hanged to show the world what
slave owners do to Negro thieves. Loud

applause nearly drowned out his last words.

Then the judge turned to Alexander. "Have you anything to say?"

Before Alexander could answer, a voice outside the courtroom shouted, "Here's Joe! Here's Joe!" Everyone turned to look.

The black man came running into the courtroom and rushed over to the colonel. He begged the colonel's forgiveness, saying that on Saturday night he had gone to visit his brother on a plantation eight miles away.

"I know I shouldn't have gone, but I hadn't seen him in such a long time. I was going to be back on Sunday, but I sprained my ankle and couldn't walk until Monday night. When I got home, I heard what had happened, and I rushed over here."

Alexander listened closely to this story. He knew Joe was trying to save him. What a brave man to return to this roomful of angry slave owners!

The judge ordered the sheriff to set Alexander free immediately. Rubbing his aching wrists, Alexander looked at the colonel.

"You've caused me a great deal of harm, and so I want a favor from you," he said. The colonel tried to turn away, but Alexander went on.

"Don't punish Joe for what he did. Let me give him a gift for his coming here to tell what happened."

The crowd in the courtroom shouted, "Yes!" and the colonel reluctantly agreed. Alexander then gave Joe twenty dollars. A short while later, the sheriff escorted Alexander to the train station and told him to get out and stay out of Columbus.

Two years later Alexander was eating dinner at a restaurant in Boston. A man who had been eyeing him for a while came up to him.

"Aren't you Alexander Ross?" the man said.

Alexander looked up, paused for a moment, and said, "Joe?"

"Yes!" the man replied. They talked for a long time, and Alexander learned that his twenty dollars had made it possible for Joe to escape. A few days after Alexander had left Columbus, Joe ran off and met his brother in the woods. They both fled North. After weeks of traveling and hiding, they reached an Underground Railroad station Alexander had told Joe about. His brother had gone all the way to Canada, but Joe had stayed in Boston.

As Alexander listened to Joe's story, he marveled at the way things had turned out. He had gone South to help the slaves. He had never dreamed that one day a slave would save *his* life.

WILLIAM STILL
Underground Agent

William Still was the author of an important book on people who escaped on the Underground Railroad.

Around Midnight

William was soaking wet that afternoon when he came home from school. One knee was bleeding and his pants legs and shirt sleeves were torn. It was thirty years before the Civil War, but slavery wasn't allowed in New Jersey. William limped home. He thought to himself, why are there so many people who hate blacks?

"What happened?" cried Sidney Still as William slowly pushed the door open.

"Nothing, Mama."

"William," she insisted, "what happened?"

His arms ached as he unbuttoned his shirt and took it off.

"Some kids pushed me off the bridge after we got out of school," he said finally.

Mrs. Still pressed her lips together. He didn't have to say anything more. She could picture what had happened. There were only a few black children in the nearly all-white school. William had been teased, yelled at, even threatened. But this was the first time anyone had actually hurt him.

She knew the scrape on his knee would heal, and she'd sew the rips in his shirt and pants, but she worried about how he felt and what he was thinking. The wound that was left when people attack you because of your skin color — well, that's something that doesn't get fixed up so easily, she thought. She gave William a long hug. Then she picked up the shirt and turned to get her sewing basket.

That night Mr. and Mrs. Still talked quietly after William had gone to sleep. He was the youngest of their children, not yet a teenager, and they thought often about the cruelty and violence he had yet to see.

"Nothing we can do to stop it, but we must help him know it's *their* meanness and not *his* fault," his father said with a quiet anger.

Levin Still, William's father, had been born a slave, but he was free now. When he was a young man, he had told his owner that he'd die before he'd stay a slave. Afraid Levin might kill himself, the owner decided to let Levin buy his own freedom. That way the owner figured he wouldn't lose Levin without payment.

It took several years, but Levin managed to get extra jobs, working day and night shifts, hardly sleeping at all, it seemed. Every time he had a little money saved, he gave it to his owner and watched as the figures were put into an account book. When Levin finally made the last payment, the owner gave him a piece of paper that said he was free. Levin couldn't read the paper, but he knew the words on it by heart.

And now his son was going to learn to read. And no white bullies were going to stop him!

"It was bound to happen sooner or later," Mrs. Still said, breaking into her husband's thoughts. But as she spoke, she had no idea that soon William was to learn an even more violent lesson.

Not too long after his trouble at the bridge, William woke with a start as a thunderclap broke overhead. He knew it was around midnight because he saw the embers glowing in the fireplace. As he listened to the rain beating on the roof, he suddenly realized there was another pounding — someone was banging on the front door. He reached the door just as his father was opening it.

Gabriel Thompson was outside with his arms around a man who was bleeding badly. Gabriel was William's brother-in-law, and he and William's sister lived nearby. Gabriel helped the wounded man into the house. William lit a candle and saw that the other man was the runaway slave who worked for old Thomas Wilkins down the road.

"A gang of slave hunters tried to kidnap him earlier tonight," said Gabriel. "Lucky Mr. Wilkins and his sisters heard the noise and ran into the room. They may be old," he said admiringly, "but one of them picked up a shovel by the fireplace and threw a pile of burning embers on the slave hunters!"

William looked wide-eyed as Gabriel continued with the story.

"That gave this poor man a chance to fight back, and those miserable hunters finally ran off. Then he managed to get to my house, but we've got to take him someplace safe, tonight." He looked at William and said, "Will you help me?"

Within minutes, William, Gabriel, and the runaway slave went back out into the dark, wet night. They made their way through the deep pine forest to a farmhouse many miles away. There they left the fugitive in the care of trusted friends and turned around to head home.

The sun was already up when William reached his house. Shivering, he changed clothes and sat down by the fireplace. His mother had a distant look in her eyes as she brought over a bowl of hot cereal. She sat down in the chair across from him, looking past him as if she could see for hundreds of miles, and began speaking.

"Peter and little Levin were so young when I had to leave them with Grandmama. Barely six and eight, they were. But I couldn't . . . I couldn't take them with me. Four children, and I had to leave two," she murmured. Her eyes filled with tears.

William listened to his mother's soft voice. He couldn't remember a time when he hadn't known this story. He knew just what his mother would say next, for she always told the story the same way.

She had been a slave in Maryland, and had run away from her owner, taking her four children with her. She had escaped North to be with her husband, William's father, in New Jersey. They had lived there secretly and happily for months, until one terrible night when slave hunters found her and took her back to Maryland. Her owner had kept her locked up in a room for months until he felt certain she'd never try to escape again.

He was wrong. Sidney Still waited until she had worked out a plan. And then one night she ran. But this time she could take only two of her children. She had to leave Peter and Levin behind.

After his mother finished her story, William was so tired he lay down to take a nap. He started to dream about the runaway. But in the dream, the slave turned into Peter and Levin. And William was running through a dark pine forest to hide them in a safe place.

When he awoke, he thought about the two brothers he had known all his life, yet had never met.

Struck by Lightning

The year was 1850, and William was now almost thirty years old. Nine years earlier, he had left his home in New Jersey and moved to Philadelphia, where he now lived with his wife, Letitia, and their two children.

William sat at his desk in the Pennsylvania Antislavery Society office, opening the afternoon mail. He had worked at the Society for a number of years, and one of his jobs was to help runaway slaves.

Helping fugitives was, of course, secret work. These were dangerous times. The letter in William's hand told of a white man who had tried to help a runaway slave and her three children escape from a southern plantation. His body had been found floating in a river, two bullets in his back. The woman and her children had been returned to their owner.

Even in Pennsylvania, a state where slavery was outlawed, helping a fugitive from another state was against the law. William knew that if he was caught he'd be arrested and put on trial. And even when he *hadn't* broken the law, there were always people who would falsely testify that he had aided in "kidnapping" a black. An innocent person could be found guilty and locked up in prison for years.

It was a warm summer day, a beautiful day, but William felt only sadness and anger as he folded up the letter he had just finished reading.

Just then two black men came into the office. William knew one of them. The other man was a stranger.

"Mr. Still," said the man William knew, "this man wants to talk with you. I don't know if" — he paused a moment — "well, he'll tell you his story, and I'll be leaving now."

William smiled at the stranger and motioned to the chair beside his desk. The man sat down nervously.

"How can I help you?" William asked.

The man stammered, "I'm . . . I'm trying to find my family. I'm from Alabama and . . . and I think my parents came North about forty years ago."

"Do you know where they lived?"

"No."

"Do you know the name of any town, or river, or city where they might have been?" asked William.

"No."

"Well, then, what *can* you tell me?"

The stranger seemed to be reaching back into childhood memories. "My little brother and I lived up here for a while, near a river, but then we went back South and my mother went away."

"What is your name?" asked William.

"Peter," the man said.

"And what is your brother's name?"

"Levin. He died a few years ago."

William looked closely at the man and then continued. "What were the names of your parents?"

"My mother's name was Sidney, my father's was Levin."

William felt as if he had been struck by lightning! Was it possible? How could he be certain? Was it a trick? Had this man been hired by slave-owners to track down runaways?

Most people wouldn't have anything to do with slave-hunting, but sadly, there were always a few, black or white, who would do anything for money.

William continued to question the man for more than an hour. Finally he said, "I think I can tell you about your family." The man looked up eagerly.

"What if I should tell you that I'm your brother?" William said.

The stranger was dumbfounded. He stared

at William and shook his head in disbelief. "It can't be," he murmured.

William said, "I've heard my mother talk about you and Levin for as long as I can remember. Our father died some years ago, but Mama still lives in New Jersey. And we have brothers and sisters living in New Jersey and in Philadelphia."

Peter just stared at him.

"You must come with me to meet our family," William continued.

William persuaded Peter to go with him to his sister Mary's house. It was evening when they arrived.

Mary held a candle up to Peter's face and gasped. "He looks just like Mama," she cried.

A few days later all the brothers and sisters set out for their mother's home in New Jersey. She was old and they planned to break the news to her gently. When they arrived, Peter was introduced as a friend. A little while later, Peter and Mrs. Still began talking.

"Are all these people your children?" he

asked, looking at the crowd in the room.

"Yes," she nodded. "I have a large family."

"How many children do you have?"

"Eighteen," she replied and then added, "Eight living, eight dead."

"But that's only sixteen," he said, confused.

The old woman sighed, "Two boys . . . I've grieved over them more than all the others put together."

At that moment, her oldest daughter came up and put her arm around her mother's shoulders.

"Mama," she said softly, "this is Peter, one of your lost boys."

Mrs. Still sat for a moment, bewildered by what was happening. Then she rose and went alone into the next room. When she returned minutes later, she went up to Peter, put her hands on his face, and began to smile and cry and cry and smile, until it seemed there could be no tears left.

As William watched his mother and brother, an idea came to him. From now on, he'd keep a logbook with full descriptions of fugitives, their family histories as best they knew them, who their owners were, where they had lived, and any other information that someday, somehow, might help bring other families back together again.

Arrested!

William kept his logbook locked in the bottom drawer of his desk at the office. He took it out from time to time to make entries. Every time a fugitive slave came through Philadelphia on the way North, William wrote the name in his book.

William entered a new name in the log. — Lear Green. She had just arrived locked in a sea chest that had been shipped to Philadelphia from Maryland! She would be staying with him and his family before heading to upstate New York.

He knew his wife, Letitia, and the children would be fascinated by her story — eighteen hours in a trunk, with just a little food and water, never knowing if she'd be caught. Who but a runaway slave would know how frightening it can be to have to sneeze! he thought.

The Stills had lived for so many years with the danger of arrest for hiding runaway slaves, that most of the time they didn't even think about the risks anymore. If you worried all the time, you'd probably never do anything.

William had several letters to read before he went home. Many fugitives wrote to him after they had passed safely through Philadelphia. One letter read:

"Mr Still,
I ar rivd on Friday evenen bot I havent eny clouse nor money please send my tronke if et has come. If my brother as well send him on for I haf a plase for him ef he ant well please dont send him for this as no plase for a sik possan. Pleas ancer this as soon as you gat et you must

*excues this bad riting for my chance wars
bot small to line this mouch,*
     John H. Dade"

William knew that in some states, slaves
were beaten, even sent to jail, for trying to
learn to read and write. Dade's last sentence
told the whole story: "You must excuse this
bad writing, for my chance was but small
to learn this much."

As he put the letter back in its envelope,
a young black boy ran into the office and
handed him a note. It read:

*"Mr. Still: Will you come down to Blood-
good's Hotel as soon as possible — as
there are three slaves here and they want
liberty. Their master is here on his way to
New York."*

William couldn't read the signature.

He raced out of the building and ran
several blocks to the office of Mr. Passmore
Williamson, a lawyer and member of the
Society, and showed him the note. Then

William headed for the hotel. If an owner brought slaves into a free state, then the slaves had a right to remain and become free. These slaves weren't runaways! If he could only reach them in time, he might help them to freedom. *If only . . . time . . . if only . . . time . . . if only . . . time . . .* the words beat out a rhythm as he ran through the streets.

When he arrived at the hotel, several black porters seemed to know why he had come before he said a word. One whispered, "They've gone to the boat!"

"What do they look like?" William panted.

"The woman is tall and dark, and she's got two little boys."

Passmore Williamson had just reached the hotel. The two men ran to the dock.

"They're on the second deck," a voice floated up from the crowd.

William and Passmore were rushing by so quickly, they didn't see who had spoken. Up the staircase the two men leaped. The decks were being cleared of visitors as the boat prepared for departure. There she was!

Leaning against a cabin wall was a nervous-looking woman with her arms around the shoulders of two young boys. On her right sat a white man with a cane in his hand.

William looked at the woman and asked, "Are you traveling?"

"Yes," she murmured.

"With whom?" She nodded toward the man with the cane.

"Does that woman belong to you, sir?" William turned to the man.

"Yes," came the swift reply.

Passmore stepped up and in a kindly voice said to the woman, "Under the laws of Pennsylvania you are entitled to your freedom because your owner brought you into the state." The woman looked frightened and hugged the two boys closer to her. Passmore continued.

"Don't be afraid. You can be as free as your owner. We will not force you to leave if you want to remain a slave. But if you lose this chance, you may never get another!"

The owner interrupted Passmore several times saying that the woman wanted to be left alone and that she was happy as she was. But, looking into her eyes, William knew how false that was.

The last bell rang for departing visitors. They had to leave. He gently touched the woman's arm and said, "Come." She immediately stepped forward with her children and followed William to the stairway. The owner rushed after her and collided with Passmore. William, the woman, and her two sons left the boat and hurried into a carriage. Passmore was still arguing with the owner.

The carriage drove through the darkened streets and William learned that the woman's name was Jane Johnson. He arranged for her to stay that first night at a friend's house. The next day she and her boys moved to his home.

William sat in his office, waiting for the trouble to begin. Starting a riot or kidnapping — he knew that Jane's owner would find someone to swear falsely that Jane was taken against her will.

He didn't have to wait long.

First, Passmore Williamson was ordered

to court to explain the whereabouts of Jane Johnson. When he came before the judge, he stated that he had no idea where she and her children were. And William knew that was true. The day after the incident on the boat, Passmore had asked only if Jane was safe. When told "Yes," he nodded and left town for a few days on business.

The judge ordered Passmore to be locked up in jail for refusing to answer the question. But how could he answer, thought William, when he really didn't know!

And then William was arrested. It was just as he had predicted. He and five porters from the hotel were charged with riot, kidnapping, and assault.

"Assault!" he fairly shouted to Letitia. "I didn't hit her owner. I never even touched him. Nobody fought. And there was no riot. Nobody did anything, either to help us or stop us!"

William was the first to go on trial. In the beginning it seemed that nobody cared about the truth. Witness after witness stated that William had forced the woman to leave the boat. They said he had shouted at people and fought his way off. Letitia sat in the courtroom angry that people were so willing to lie.

Then came William's lawyer, Charles Gibbons. As he finished questioning a witness on William's side, a woman wearing a dark veil entered the courtroom by the rear door. Nobody seemed to notice. Until, that is, Mr. Gibbons called his next witness.

"Jane Johnson!" he said loudly. A low murmur swept through the room as the woman in the veil walked to the witness chair.

"Nobody forced me to do anything," she said in a voice so low that the judge had to lean forward to hear her. "I don't want to go back. I could go now," she paused and glanced quickly at her owner, "but I'd rather die than go back!"

William was found not guilty.

Two of the porters from the hotel were not so lucky. They were convicted of assaulting Jane Johnson's owner, even though they hadn't been near him. They were locked up in jail for a week.

And Passmore Williamson suffered the worst punishment. He remained in jail for three months because the judge hadn't believed him when he said he didn't know where Jane Johnson was staying.

There was no way to explain these twists of fate, thought William. When you work in the antislavery movement in these terrible times, it seems justice in the courtroom is as much a question of luck as truth.

Hide the Books

Early one October morning in 1859, William opened the newspaper, and the headlines screamed out:

"Siege at Harpers Ferry!"

"Old Brown on the Attack!"

For a moment he was stunned. He knew John Brown, a long-time abolitionist. And he knew that Brown had had plans to free slaves someplace in Virginia.

William hadn't thought the plan could succeed, and he had hoped that Brown would have abandoned the idea. He read the paper quickly. The story was brief. No one knew yet what really had happened. When he went home that evening, he and Letitia talked long into the night about John Brown and his powerful desire to end slavery.

"His heart is good and his mind is good, but the plan is just wrong," William kept saying over and over. "How can a small group of armed men ever think they can free slaves without many, many people getting hurt or killed!"

Letitia looked at William. Their house had been a station on the Underground Railroad for so many years, she could hardly remember a day when someone wasn't staying over on the way North.

"We all fight this battle as best we can." And then she added quietly, "John Brown did what he had to."

The next days were busy at the office. People kept flocking in, wanting to know the latest news about Harpers Ferry.

"I read that southerners are arming themselves and organizing small fighting bands," said one.

"Where will it lead?" asked another.

"War, that's where," a third said, as he pointed to a newspaper article. "It says here that John Brown believes there's going to be a war over slavery!"

"Did you hear that they've arrested a dozen people in the antislavery movements in Boston and New York!" said another.

And then came the news that soldiers under the command of Colonel Robert E. Lee had wounded and captured Brown. At least ten of Brown's men had been killed, and the U.S. government planned to put John Brown on trial for treason. Everyone knew he'd be convicted.

Within days came an even more frightening story for William. The newspapers reported that the notebooks of one of Brown's men had been found. One entry read, "Wrote William Still Wednesday." William caught his breath. He hadn't been involved in the Harpers Ferry raid, but if officials believed he had . . . he didn't want to think about what might happen.

That very afternoon he began to pack up

his Underground Railroad notebooks. William had kept his vow the day Peter and their mother were reunited. He had filled many notebooks with the stories of fugitive slaves who had passed through Philadelphia. Now it had become very dangerous to keep these books. If they ever were found, William knew they'd be evidence that he had helped hundreds of runaway slaves. And then he, too, might be put on trial.

William tried to find a hiding place for the notebooks. He kept changing the spot, never certain it was really safe. At night, he and Letitia waited nervously for a knock on the door, for an official who would arrest William and take him away.

Just when they thought the danger had passed, a tired, sore, and hungry man appeared at their door. One of John Brown's men! They quickly hid him in a basement room and sent the children off to stay with relatives. If the army tracked this man down, there might be shooting inside William's house. Late that night, William gave the man some money and brought him to another safe house in the city. The next morning the man left for Canada.

It took several weeks before William found a safe place for the notebooks. He confided his secret to Letitia:

"The Lebanon Cemetery, that's where! My stories of people's lives are now side by side with the bones of the dead."

Letitia smiled. "Somehow I don't think either group would mind," she said.

Four more people involved with John Brown passed through the Still house over the next weeks. And each time, William and Letitia risked danger to feed and clothe them and give them money for the long trip to Canada.

No one ever came to arrest William.

Less than two years after William hid his books, the Civil War began. The great and bloody and terrible war that John Brown had predicted would happen if the slaves were not freed.

William's notebooks remained hidden for the four long war years. At last, the fighting was over. In December, 1865, William opened his newspaper to a thrilling headline:

SLAVERY IS DEAD!

He read the story about the Thirteenth Amendment to the United States Constitution, the amendment that abolished slavery. He sat thinking about all the people he had met through the years — all those who had escaped from their owners.

And he remembered his notebooks. Had they survived the war? Mice like to chew paper to make bedding. Had they eaten their way through the hundreds of pages?

"Right where I had hidden them!" he told Letitia that evening. "They're all there!"

"What will you do with them now?" she asked.

It was years before William had an answer. In May, 1871, the Pennsylvania Antislavery Society held its final meeting. At the meeting, the members asked William to organize his Underground Railroad notebooks and publish them as a book.

In 1872, *The Underground Railroad* by William Still sold thousands of copies. William was delighted. He hoped that former slaves might find clues in the pages of his book that would help them find each other in real life.

One night at dinner he said to his own family, "With this book, everyone will know of the incredible bravery of the slaves who escaped to freedom." Then he looked at his children. "You've met many of these people. And you must tell their stories to your children, and they to their children. For the world must never forget such courage."

LEESHA BOS*
Nazi Fighter

*Leesha's name was originally Hava Bornstein. When she joined the Resistance, she changed her name to Leesha Bos.

Hava Bornstein became Elisabeth Bos when she needed false identity papers during World War II.

"We're Trapped!"

Hava Bornstein, a Dutch Jew, had been working at the Jewish Invalid Hospital in Amsterdam for almost a year when the announcement came:

"The hospital will be evacuated tomorrow, March first!"

Just eight words, but Hava knew they meant death for many people. Perhaps herself.

As she sat in her room, Hava thought about the last three years. Only three years since the Nazis invaded Holland on that terrible Friday morning in May, 1940 — and yet it felt like forever. Days and nights filled with the sounds of screaming sirens, gun fire in the streets, the pounding of army boots on the pavement, and always the planes flying overhead.

She talked about the announcement with Ann and Marge, other nurses who worked with her.

"Who knows if the Germans will really deport everyone this time," Ann said, not expecting an answer. "You remember the other rumors."

The others nodded. They had had this discussion many times before when they had heard that the Germans would round up all the patients and workers and send everyone to concentration camps.

"Not too long ago, my little brother Jackie asked my father if a concentration camp was where people went on summer vacation," Hava said. "How can you expect a five-year-old child to understand that the Nazis are rounding up people just because they are Jews?" She paused. "I'm almost twenty-one, and I can't understand it."

"Well, are you going to leave the hospital

before the Germans come?" Marge asked.

"Yes, of course, aren't you?" Ann said.

Marge nodded yes, and so did the others.

But Hava said, "So many of the patients are crippled or paralyzed. If the Germans do come this time, they'll arrive tomorrow morning. If none of us stays, who'll take care of the patients through the night? They'll be completely helpless."

Hava knew what she had to do.

At eight o'clock, the doors of the hospital were locked. Hava was one of the few nurses remaining in the building. She talked with the others about a plan. If the Germans came to evacuate the hospital, the staff would try to escape from the roof to the next building. If that was impossible, there was a hiding place with blankets, food and water, and candles under a trapdoor in the floor of the hospital synagogue.

A little after eight thirty the next morning, the lookout person stationed on the roof came running in.

"The Germans are surrounding the building!" he shouted.

Hava ran up to the roof with five others. Looking down, they saw rows of trucks around the entire block. German soldiers stood with their rifles and bayonets drawn. Escape over the roof was impossible. The six ran down the stairs to the synagogue, but the Nazis were already in the building. No one could reach the hiding place.

"We're trapped!" one of the nurses cried.

The Germans began issuing orders:

"Prepare the patients for transport!"

"Move!"

"Into this van and be quick about it!"

By three o'clock in the afternoon, the hundreds of patients were all on the trucks. The staff was then ordered to join them.

Hava stood in the lobby looking through the front doors of the hospital. They were doors leading to death . . . or maybe. . . .

She began to roll up her white nurse's apron so that it wouldn't show under her coat. Laura, one of the other nurses, whispered, "What are you going to do?"

"Shhh! Don't talk or you'll draw attention to me."

"Please take me with you!" Laura begged.

"It's very risky," Hava whispered. "I may be shot. I can't be responsible for you."

But Laura insisted.

"Then just follow me exactly and don't say anything," Hava said as she walked toward the hospital doors. Once on the street they walked quickly past the trucks filled with patients and staff.

"Where are you going? Halt!" a voice shouted.

"Don't turn around and don't start running," Hava whispered. "Pretend you haven't heard anything."

They crossed the street into the middle of the traffic. Hidden by cars and trucks, they began walking a little faster. When there were no more soldiers in sight, they began to run. And they ran until it felt as if their lungs would burst.

That night, Hava slept for twelve hours. Exhausted, but still alive.

In the Resistance

In April, 1943, the Nazi commandant in Amsterdam announced that Jewish people still left in the city were to be deported immediately. The roundup began in earnest. The rattling of trucks over cobblestoned streets, the clicking of bayonets, the pounding on doors, a sharp order to move quickly — daily sounds of terror.

A short time after her escape, Hava had begun working again, this time at the Netherland Israelite Hospital (N.I.Z.). The Nazis hadn't yet evacuated all the Jewish hospitals, and N.I.Z. was filled with patients, many of whom were trying to escape deportation, at least for a while.

One day Hava brought food and medication to a patient who was under special police guard. She was told the patient had been shot while trying to escape from a group of German soldiers. As she set up the tray, he began speaking to her.

"They caught me this time, and I don't think I'll make it."

Hava noticed his name as she looked at his chart. "You'll be fine, Peter. The doctors are doing all they can."

"You don't understand," he said hoarsely. "Who will continue my work in the Resistance? The Resistance organization can't reach me here. And besides," he looked at her intently as he continued, "the Nazis want me to live only so they can torture me so they can learn what we're doing."

Hava gave him his medication, and he continued whispering, his breath short and rasping.

"One of the other nurses told me about your escape from the Jewish Invalid Hospital

. . . you know how to think and act quickly . . . will you help in the Resistance? . . . think about it before you answer . . . your life will be in danger." He paused. "Whatever you decide, I'll give you the information now in case I don't last the night."

Then he whispered an address and the password, "The tulips are red."

As Hava walked back past the police guard, she knew this was one decision she couldn't talk about with anyone. Absolute secrecy was necessary, or many people might be in danger.

A few days later Hava went to Peter's room. Doctors and nurses were rushing in and out so often that she was able to slip past the German guard unnoticed. But there was no way to talk with Peter. She caught his eye and nodded slightly. He understood and smiled. A few days later he died.

Hava began her work for the Resistance. Hundreds of Jews were being hidden in Christian homes throughout Holland. The Resistance made all the arrangements. Hava was part of the system in the hospital.

Whenever a patient wanted to go into hiding, Hava contacted the Resistance. During visiting hours, a "relative" or "friend" would come to the hospital to see the patient. At the end of the visit, the patient would mingle in the departing crowd, leave the hospital, and go to an agreed-upon address with the "visitor." Many children as well as adults left the hospital this way through Hava's work.

Then the dreaded raid happened. The Germans swept into the hospital early one morning to evacuate patients and some staff.

"All nurses who worked at the Jewish Invalid Hospital report downstairs immediately!"

This time Hava had a chance to hide. She wouldn't voluntarily give herself up to the Nazis.

The order was repeated. The announcer added, "If you don't come immediately, we will take other nurses as hostages!"

If she could protect herself, she would. But she wouldn't let another nurse be deported in her place. Hava came out of the closet where she had hidden, went downstairs and climbed into one of the waiting trucks. They were driven to a train station for deportation. The Germans were wasting no time in getting rid of this truckload of Jews — the trains were already there.

As they were set to depart, a Nazi soldier suddenly shouted out four names and ordered these people off the train. Hava knew them, for they had all worked in one of the special units at N.I.Z. Two nurses left the train and walked over to the officer. The soldier called out the other names again. No answer.

They must have gotten away! Hava realized, and she jumped to the ground and went up to the soldier.

"I am Lilly Bromet," she said. Could he see her knees shaking? Would he ask to see her identity card? Would he kill her on the spot if he discovered the lie? Her hands shook as she put her knapsack on her back.

The train engines started up, and she and the other two nurses were told to get into one of the trucks. An oversight, an accident, a miracle, but the Nazi officer in charge hadn't asked to see her identity card!

The three were returned to the hospital that night. Once again she had escaped deportation. Hava felt like a cat with nine lives who'd already used up two of them.

A New Name

Shortly after her narrow escape, Hava had to go into hiding. Jews were being rounded up by the thousands. Friends in the Resistance hid her in a tiny room. They'd bring her a tray of food at night.

The Resistance was planning to get her a false identity card. They could steal blank cards from the City Registry, but only a few could be removed at a time without the Germans noticing. Waiting was hard. She hated being cooped up.

What to do with the long hours of lock-in? Hava slept badly. She tossed much of

the night, thinking of her family—her brother
Paul, just a few years younger than she;
Jackie, the little one; and her parents. All
had been caught by the Nazis and deported
to a concentration camp. First her father,
then her mother and Jackie together, and
now finally Paul. Who knew where they'd
be sent? Hava cried mostly when she slept.
She'd wake up, her face wet with tears.
During the days, she sat and waited. And
waited.

Finally one day, Jules, the good friend
who was hiding Hava, arrived with the new
card. Picture, fingerprints, official stamp.
And a new name. Elisabeth Bos, Leesha for
short. Hava Bornstein was dead, gone, van-
ished — whatever the Nazis wanted to think.
From now on, she was Leesha Bos. Hava
Bornstein had had the letter "J" on her old
card, standing for "Jew." Elisabeth Bos didn't.
According to her new papers, she wasn't
Jewish.

Leesha received her instructions from
the Resistance: Forget your old name; forget
your family; make up a new history, where

you went to school, who your family is, and memorize it all very carefully.

But how do you forget? How do you stop thinking about Friday night dinner at home with your family? About silly games you played with your little brother? About long talks with your parents? About secrets shared with friends? How?

Work helped. And Leesha threw herself into the Resistance work. Packages were delivered to her new home to be forwarded on to someone else. A package would come with a sender's address written on it. She'd change the wrapper, deduct ten from the number on the original sender's address, which was the code for finding the new address, and mail it on. Sometimes she'd secretly meet another Resistance worker and deliver the package in person.

One day she met her new Underground contact, Fritz van Dongen. Fritz's real name was Reinier van Kampenhout. His Resistance group had raided police stations and Nazi-controlled offices to steal ration and identity cards. They had also blown up bridges and railroad tracks.

Leesha and Fritz became close friends as well as co-workers. In these terrible times, she thought, it's wonderful to have a friend you care about and who cares about you.

One day someone in the Resistance came to her door with an urgent message.

"It's an emergency, Leesha! Our friend has gone on vacation. You must go to the city of Leiden quickly. They need you."

Our friend? On vacation? That meant Fritz, but he wouldn't go on vacation. The Nazis had captured him! That was the dreadful message.

Leesha walked miles in the pouring rain to Leiden. She went straight to her contact and was given another address to go to. When she walked in, she was introduced by the one person she knew.

"This is Leesha Bos. I sent for her. She worked closely with Fritz and knew him well," a man named Eddy said. He turned to Leesha. "Victor will tell you the rest."

Victor spoke the terrible words. "Fritz and his wife were picked up yesterday when the Germans raided his home. He had been taking care of nearly two hundred Jews and non-Jews who are in hiding."

Leesha held her breath as Victor continued. "He brought them food, ration cards, rent money. Leesha," he stared at her intently, *"you must take his place."*

Everyone looked at her. She sat silent and overwhelmed.

"How will I find these people?" she finally murmured.

"Of course Fritz kept no records. But we know of six names," Victor said. "Somehow you will find the others."

She began the next day to locate the *onderduikers*. That's what they were called — people who hid "underground" to escape from the Nazis. She discovered new names in all sorts of ways. She'd talk to storeowners and ask if anyone had seen Fritz. Sometimes there was a blunt answer, "No." Other times shopkeepers would talk a little, saying that Fritz was missed by many people. Leesha took that as a clue that perhaps they knew more. She'd return the next day and coax any further information out of them.

Often the people who hid *onderduikers* knew of others who were also being helped. In less than three weeks, Leesha learned the names of about a hundred and fifty people in hiding. They would anxiously await her visits, not only for the life-saving food and rations she brought, but also for the comfort of her company. For many of them, Leesha was the only person from the outside world with whom they talked.

And then one day Victor asked, "Would you like to assist us in a 'special event' soon? We can use you."

Whistle a Tune

A special event! Leesha wondered what it could be. She knew that she would be told only what she had to know. This was standard procedure for everyone who worked in the Resistance. In this way, there would be a limit to what you could reveal if you were caught and tortured.

Conditions throughout Holland were getting worse. Dutch non-Jews between the ages of seventeen and fifty were being rounded up and deported to Germany to slave labor camps. And the Germans were bribing people with desperately needed money, food, and extra rations to reveal the hiding places of the *onderduikers*.

Food was so scarce many people were dying of starvation, particularly the very young and the old. Leesha even had to organize the secret burial of an elderly man, one of her *onderduikers*.

One night Victor told Leesha that she'd get a message the next day with her instructions. In the morning she learned the reason for the "special event." The Resistance was very low on money for supplies for all the people it was helping.

"We're going to rob the Rotterdamse Bank at noon today," Victor said.

The fourteen Resistance members at the meeting listened closely to the plan. Victor looked at Leesha and a woman named Julie and continued.

"You two will be lookouts. You'll stand across the street from the bank and talk like friends meeting during lunchtime. If you see the police or Nazis approaching, you'll wave and shout 'hello' to Hans. He'll be in front of the bank watching you."

The meeting broke up and everyone left separately. Leesha rode her bike to the bank and waited for Julie to arrive. When she came, they stood chatting as they leaned against their bikes. Across the street they saw the others enter the bank. Hans remained outside just as Victor had said he would.

It was hard to nod and laugh and talk when you were so nervous. Through a big smile, Julie whispered, "How much longer, do you think?"

"Soon. It must be soon, because it's only supposed to take ten minutes," answered Leesha.

And then, finally, it was over. They saw the others leave the bank, one at a time. When everyone was gone, Leesha and Julie got on their bikes and rode off in opposite directions.

Leesha felt enormous relief to be pedaling home. Then, as she started down one street, she saw two German trucks at the end of the block. The Nazis had roped off the street and were searching everybody, checking their identification papers.

Now she was in real danger! She had a small gun in her belt and some stolen ration cards and blank identity cards inside her blouse. They'd arrest her for sure. She quickly turned her bike around and rode against the traffic.

"Halt! Halt!" screamed one of the German officers. He jumped on a bike and raced after her.

Leesha was desperate. She began to whistle the Resistance signal, the first four notes of Beethoven's Fifth Symphony. If there were friends of the Resistance in the crowd, they'd whistle back the next four notes.

"Ba ba ba bom . . ."

"Ba ba ba bom," came the answering whistle! The traffic parted down the center and let her pass.

Then she heard a crash of metal, the scraping of bikes, shouts and curses. As she reached a cross-street, she turned to glance back. It seemed as if everyone had closed up the center path after she had ridden through. The German officer was trapped in a pile of bikes and people! All she could see were his arms waving as he frantically tried to climb out of the mess and continue the chase.

She rode up and down different side streets until she felt certain that no one was following her, and then she rode home.

That night everyone got together to talk about the "special event." Victor reenacted what had happened inside the bank.

"'In the name of the Prince of Orange,'" he exclaimed, showing everyone how he had stuck a gun in the bank manager's ribs, "'raise your hands!' The man was so frightened, he stood there with his hands up and sang the national anthem! When we were ready to leave, I told them, 'This is not a robbery. It is a raid organized by the Resistance to help Dutch people hiding from the Nazis. Better this money comes to us than to the Germans!'" he finished triumphantly.

That night Leesha dreamt again about her family. If only she could whistle *them* to safety.

An End and a Beginning

In 1945 the Allied forces of Britain, the United States, and Canada swept into Holland to help liberate that battered country.

The Allies and the Nazis were battling in the countryside. One night Leesha and several of her friends were on a Resistance mission. Their car had run out of gas and they were stranded on a dark and lonely road. In the distance they could hear the sounds of gunfire. Would a German or an Allied car pass them first? Their lives might depend on the answer.

And that's when they met Captain Isaac Rose, a Canadian army officer. He helped them get gas that night to complete their mission and later celebrated with them on liberation day, May 5, 1945.

When the victory parties ended, the Dutch people began the work of rebuilding. Holland was out of gas, out of electricity, and out of food. The Germans had destroyed much of the country. It was as if the heart of many cities had been bombed out. And the hearts of many people as well.

Leesha searched for information about her family. She, along with thousands of others like her, poured over Red Cross lists to find news of relatives.

Then one terrible day Leesha learned what she didn't want to know. Her father, mother, Paul, and Jackie had all been killed in German concentration camps in Auschwitz and Sobibor. She was the only Bornstein left. And even Hava Bornstein was "dead." Leesha Bos of the Dutch Resistance was the survivor.

Postscript

In 1947, two years after the war had ended, Leesha flew to Canada to marry Isaac Rose, the same Captain Rose who had helped her on that deserted road in the Dutch country-side.

For many years, Leesha didn't want to think about the terrible time of the German occupation of Holland. She was rebuilding her life. Finally, it was her son's interest in what his mother had done, what she had lived through, that convinced her to tell her own story. She wrote that story in a book called *The Tulips Are Red* — the password into the Resistance and the password to sharing with the world the experiences of Leesha Bos, Nazi Fighter.

Leesha Rose now lives in Israel with her husband Captain Rose. *The Tulips Are Red* describes her experiences during World War II and the Nazi occupation of Holland.

Step Back in Time With
📖 SCHOLASTIC BIOGRAPHY

True stories about important men and women in American history!

☐ **40639-6 The Death of Lincoln:** A Picture History of the Assassination
President Lincoln dreamed of his own death. Three weeks later, he was shot in a theater. The sad and chilling story of Lincoln's death, and what happened afterward.

☐ **40512-8 The Defenders**
Tecumseh was only six when he saw his father shot. Osceola was unjustly imprisoned. Cochise's people were sent to a reservation. The tragic stories of three American Indian heroes.

☐ **40933-6 The First Woman Doctor**
"Go home where women belong!" shouted the angry crowd. A woman doctor was unheard of in 1840. But Elizabeth Blackwell followed her dream and became the *first!*

☐ **40640-X Freedom Train: The Story of Harriet Tubman**
Harriet Tubman escaped slavery, but never forgot her people. She risked her life daily to help hundreds of others to freedom.

☐ **41342-2 They Led the Way: Fourteen American Women**
The first woman to run for president...a daring reporter who went around the world alone...a freed slave who wrote poetry...these great women made history—by doing just what they wanted to do!

☐ **40488-1 The Wright Brothers at Kitty Hawk**
Orville and Wilbur Wright had a dream that one day men would fly. On December 17, 1903, their dream came true!

Available wherever you buy books, or use the coupon below.
$2.50 each.

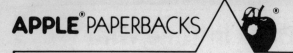